A POCKETFUL OF GAMES W

COUNTERS

Contents

Written by Ruth Thomson
Illustrated by Clare Beaton

Hippo Books
Scholastic Publications Ltd.
London

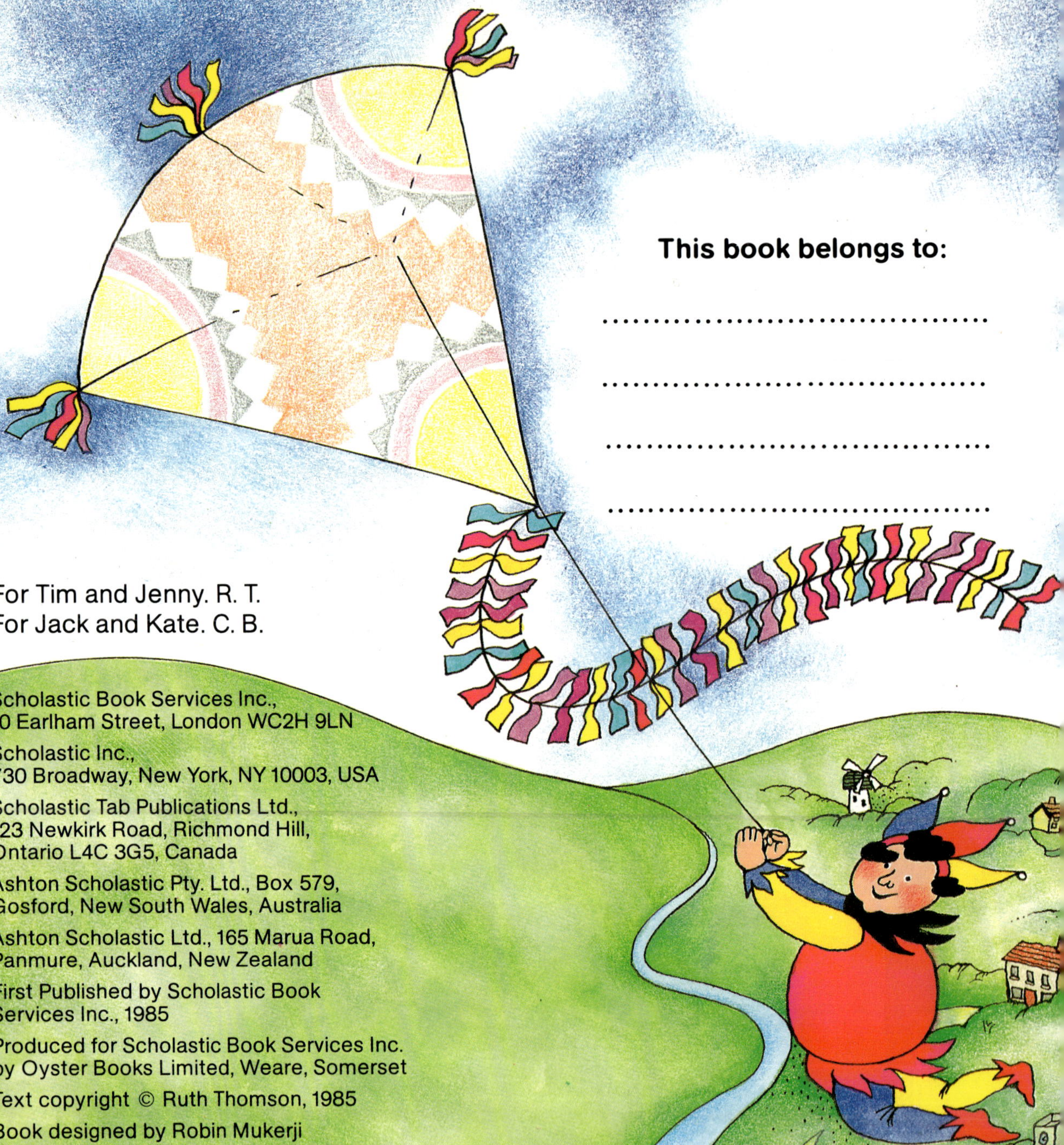

This book belongs to:

....

....

....

....

For Tim and Jenny. R. T.
For Jack and Kate. C. B.

Scholastic Book Services Inc.,
10 Earlham Street, London WC2H 9LN

Scholastic Inc.,
730 Broadway, New York, NY 10003, USA

Scholastic Tab Publications Ltd.,
123 Newkirk Road, Richmond Hill,
Ontario L4C 3G5, Canada

Ashton Scholastic Pty. Ltd., Box 579,
Gosford, New South Wales, Australia

Ashton Scholastic Ltd., 165 Marua Road,
Panmure, Auckland, New Zealand

First Published by Scholastic Book
Services Inc., 1985

Produced for Scholastic Book Services Inc.
by Oyster Books Limited, Weare, Somerset

Book designed by Robin Mukerji

ISBN 0 590 70428 1

Made and Printed by L.E.G.O., Vicenza, Italy
Filmset in Helvetica Series by Capital Letters Ltd.

For starters

This is a book of games to play with counters like these. Some of the games are old and some are brand new; some of them are easy and some are harder. Some are games you can play on the pages of this book and some are games you can make for yourself.

For making the games you need:
- some coloured crayons or felt-tipped pens
- a pair of scissors
- some paper and some stiff card

Who starts?

There are several ways to decide who is first to play.

If there are only two of you playing, put a counter in one hand and hold out both fists like this.

If your friend chooses the fist with the counter then he or she starts. If your friend chooses the empty fist, then you start.

If there are three or four players, put three or four different coloured counters into a cup and, with your eyes shut, each take one. The player who picks the yellow counter starts.

How to flip counters

The vital thing you need to know, in order to play the games in the first half of the book, is how to flip counters. Practise on a hard, flat surface.

Hold one counter like this. If you have one counter which is bigger than the rest, use that. It is known as the flipper.

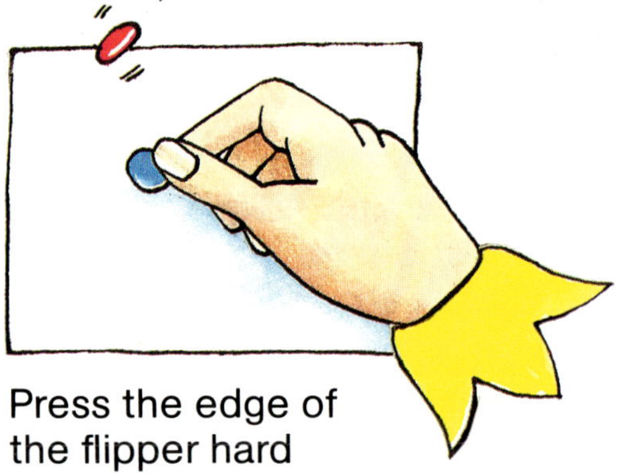

Press the edge of the flipper hard against the edge of another counter. The other counter should flip up into the air.

Pond splash (for one or more players)

How to play

Put a counter on any of the frogs and try to flip it on to either a lily or a lily pad. Once you think you can do it easily, aim for one particular lily pad. Also practise aiming from different positions off the page.

If you want, score 10 points each time you land on a lily pad and 20 points each time you land on a flower. See how high your score is after ten flips and try to improve your score each time you play.

Make sure the book is really flat before you start playing, otherwise the counters may move.

Flip for the top
(for one or more players)

Use the board opposite for flipping practice. Flip counters from the coloured circle. What is the highest score you can get in ten flips?

Climb high
(for one or more players)

When your aim is quite good, try this game. Cut a piece of paper in half lengthwise and tape the two halves together to make a long strip like a ladder. Draw lines across it to make the rungs and number each division. Number them in tens, as shown, or in fives or even in hundreds!

How to play

- Take turns to flip five counters from the starting block. Add up the score each counter makes to find your total score.
- If a counter does not land on the ladder, flip again until it does.
- If a counter lands on a line between two scores, count the higher score.

100
100
50
50
20
20
25
25
10
10
15
15
5
5
5
5

Easy egg flip
(for two or more players)

Arrange a pile of books and an empty egg box like this; the pile of books should be just a bit higher than the box. Number each of the egg box holes.

How to play

- Take turns to flip six counters each from on top of the books into the egg box.
- Count your total after you have flipped all six.
- The winner is the one with the highest score after three rounds.
- If a counter misses the egg box, it becomes a 'dead' counter and is out of that round.

Tricky egg flip
(for two or more players)

Keep the same arrangement as for the previous game, but ignore the numbers in the egg box holes.

How to play

- Take turns to flip six counters each from the top of the books into the egg box.
- The idea is to flip one counter into each hole on your turn. The first person to do so wins.
- If a counter misses the egg box completely, flip it again.

Counter race
(for two or more players)

This is a good game to play on a path or in the playground. Make a chalk line to mark the start of the track and another, several metres away, to mark the finish.

Put your counters on the starting line and, on the count of three, flip them as fast as possible along the track. The winner is the first person whose counter goes over the finishing line.

Cover the counter
(for two or more players)

This is a good, simple party game, but is just as much fun for two people. You may even enjoy playing it on your own. It's really tricky!

How to play

- Cover a counter with kitchen foil and put it at the bottom of a bucket or bowl full of water.
- Take turns to drop counters into the water and try to cover the shiny one. The player who covers it first is the winner.
- If you're playing by yourself, time how long, or count how many counters, it takes to cover the shiny counter.

Happy landings
(for two or more players)

In this game, you are a helicopter pilot. Your job is to land your helicopter safely on the oil rig.
You have five helicopters (counters) to practise with.

How to play

- Start with all your helicopters on dry land (an agreed point off the page). Flip them in turn. Try to land on the oil rig landing platform. Score as shown.
- If a helicopter lands in the sea or crashes into the tower, it is lost.
- If a helicopter lands only partly on the landing platform, count the score for the platform.
- If a helicopter lands on a line between two scores, count the higher score.
- The ace pilot is the one with the most points after all the helicopters have been flipped.
- If you want to make the game even more difficult, put an empty matchbox in the centre of the landing platform.
  Only helicopters which land inside it score. Score 50 points for each successful landing.

100
50
25

Black holes
(for one or more players)

Can you launch your spaceship to the planets without it falling into the black holes and disappearing forever?

How to play

- Take turns to flip a counter from the launch pad on earth. Score 50 points every time you land on a planet (even if only partly).
- Take away 50 points if you fall into a black hole.
- Flip again if you land in space.

Tiddlywinks

(for two or more players)

This is one of the best-known games you can play with counters. The idea is to flip counters on to the numbered sections of the board and score points. The first player to reach a total of 100 points is the winner.

Boards

The board on the opposite page shows one possible layout for a tiddlywinks board. Put an egg cup on the centre circle if you want to make the game more difficult.

You could easily invent your own boards, based either on a square or on a circle. These are a few ideas for inspiration.

The overall size should be about 18cm by 18cm. If you draw a circle, it should be at least 15cm across the width.

5
5
10
10
50
10
10
5
5

Double or quits (for two or more players)

Here's another kind of tiddlywink game, where your aim needs to be even better than usual.

You can either play on this board or make a bigger one of your own on some card. If you prefer, make up your own scores and instructions and divide the circles into larger or smaller segments.

How to play

- You each need six small counters and a big one to flip with (or an extra small one). Keep paper and pencil handy for writing down the scores. Lay the book flat on a table.
- Take turns flipping the counters on to the board from an agreed point on the table.

How to score

- If a counter lands right inside a segment, either note down the score or follow the instruction.
- If a counter lands on a line between two numbers, count the higher number.
- If a counter lands on a line between two instructions, don't follow either of them. This counter becomes 'dead'.
- If a counter lands between a number and an instruction, follow the instruction.
- The winner is the person with the highest score after all the counters have been flipped.

10
double your opponent's score
7
your opponent loses all points
4
double your own score
5
lose all your points
lose half your points
6
miss a turn
8
double your own score
1
have another turn
9
20

Shove ha'penny (for two players)

Before you can play this, you will need to make a shove ha'penny board. Use a piece of very thick cardboard or, better still, ask an adult to cut you a piece of wood the right size.

Rule lines in the positions shown below – the sizes are only guide-lines; it won't matter if your board is slightly bigger or smaller. However, it is important that a counter fits easily between two of the lines as shown below.

Once the board is made, you're ready to play. Gather a store of sixteen counters each for keeping score and an extra counter for playing with.

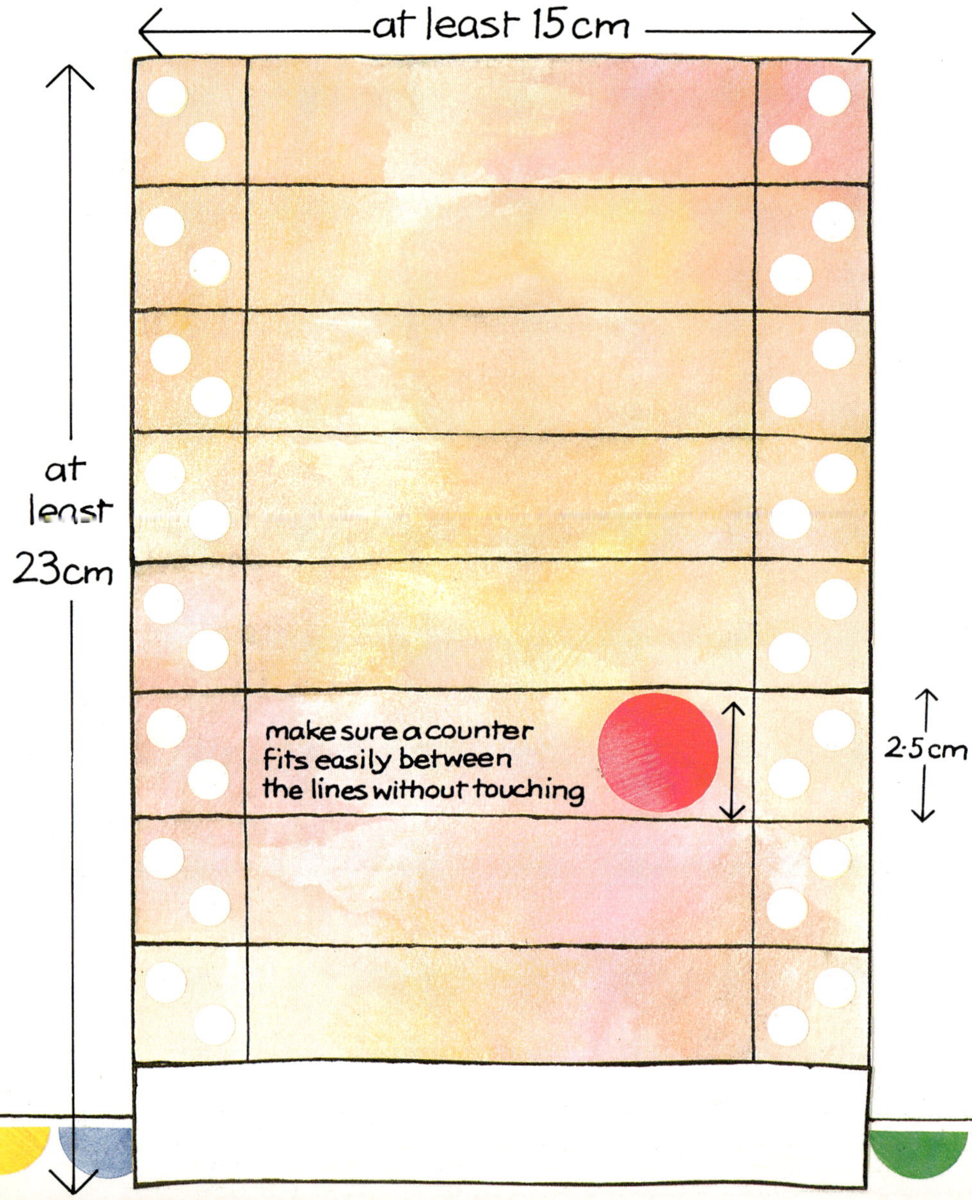

How to play

- Put the board on a table, with the edge of the board along the edge of the table. Put a heavy book behind it to keep it steady.
- Put a counter half over the edge of the board and push it with the palm of your hand.
- If it lands right inside a strip without touching any lines, cover one of the circles beside it with a counter from your store. Then have another turn.
- If a counter lands on a line, that is the end of your turn.
- The first player to cover all the circles on his or her side, wins.

Line up for dinner (for two players)

The jester's cats and dogs are very hungry, but he won't feed them unless they line up in straight rows for their own food. Tonight it's fish pie for the cats and thick stew for the dogs!

Play this game to see whether the cats or the dogs get their dinner first. You each need four counters of your own colour. Choose whether to be the cats or the dogs and put your counters on your animals to start.

How to play

- Take turns to move one counter one square forwards, backwards or sideways (but *not* diagonally). The square you move to must be empty.
- You have to move every time it is your turn, even if your move helps the other player.
- The four cats or dogs to get into a straight, unbroken line (either up and down, acrosswise or diagonally) first, can have their scrumptious dinner!

Into battle! (for two players)

The red knights are going to war against the green knights. Decide which side you will be and put eight counters of your own colour on your knights to start.
Let the battle begin!

How to play

- Take turns to move one counter.
- *Either:* move one step at a time in any direction along a line;
  or: capture an enemy by jumping over one of your own knights on to an enemy knight.
  This is how you start the game.
- Remove any captured knights (counters) from the board.
- The first army of knights to capture or block their enemy so they can no longer move is the winner.

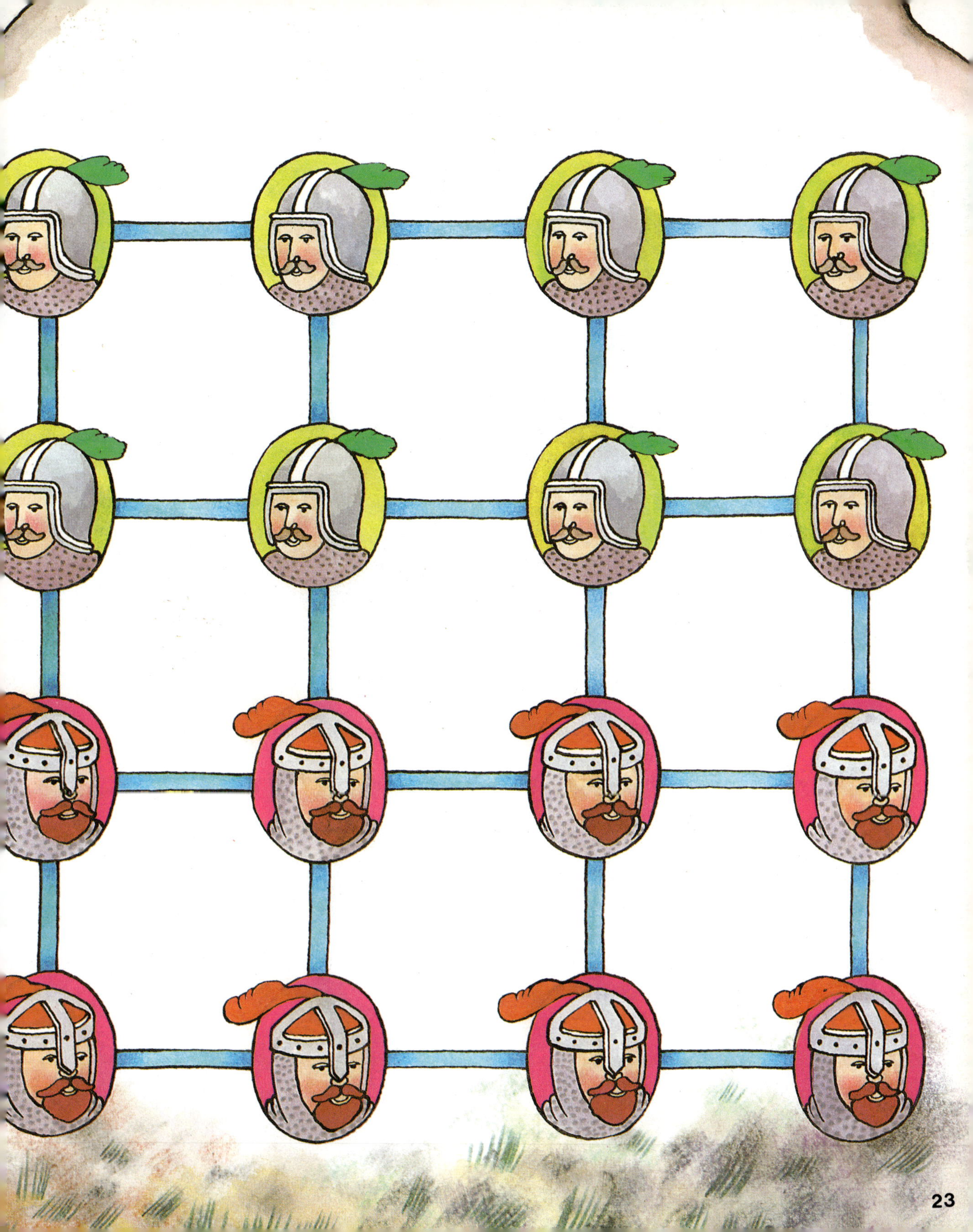

Twiddleums

(for two to six players)

This is an old board game which is trickier to play than it looks!

Each put a counter on one of the starting circles. If only two of you are playing, use three counters each. If three of you are playing, use two counters each.

If four or more are playing, use only one counter each.

How to play

- Take turns to move a counter to a circle with a number either one *higher* or one *lower* than the circle your counter is in. For example, if your counter is on a number 4 circle, it can move to a number 3 circle or a number 5 circle, but not to a number 1, 2 or 6 circle.
- Your first move is always to a number 1 circle and your second move always to a number 2 circle.
- The circle you want to move to must be empty. If you can't move, you lose a turn.
- The first person to get a counter (or all his or her counters) home is the winner.

Start for BLUE
Finish for BLACK
Start for WHITE
Finish for GREEN
Start for RED
Finish for YELLOW
Start for BLACK
Finish for BLUE
Start for GREEN
Finish for WHITE
Start for YELLOW
Finish for RED

The tiger and the lambs
(for two players)

One player has seven counters. These are the lambs. The other player has only one counter, of a different colour. This is the tiger. The tiger starts at the tip of the triangle.

How to play

- The player with the lambs puts them down, one at a time, in alternate moves with the tiger.
- The lambs cannot move from their positions until all seven have been put on the board. Then they can move one at a time, one step at a time, along the marked lines to any empty circle including the tiger's.
- Only the tiger can capture. He takes the lambs by jumping over them on to an empty circle.
- The tiger wins if he captures so many lambs that they have no chance of cornering him.
- The lambs win if they succeed in pinning the tiger to a spot, so he can no longer move.

Six tricky puzzles

Arrange your counters like this to start each puzzle.

1

2

3

4

Arrange 6 counters like this. Now move only <u>one</u> to make two rows with 4 counters in each.

5

Once you've done the puzzle above, this one should be easy! Make a square with 12 counters, like this. Now, using the same counters, make another square with 5 counters on each side.

6

Finally, here's a trick to play on your friends. Ask them to balance a counter on the edge of a piece of paper or a pound note. When they give up, show them how!

Answers

1

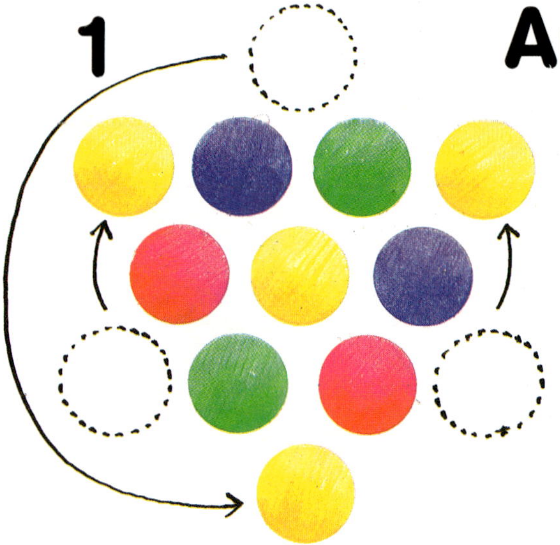

Move the 3 yellow counters like this and there you are – the triangle is upside-down.

2

Sneaky, eh? Move the top middle counter to the bottom and push up the middle row with it until the counters line up.

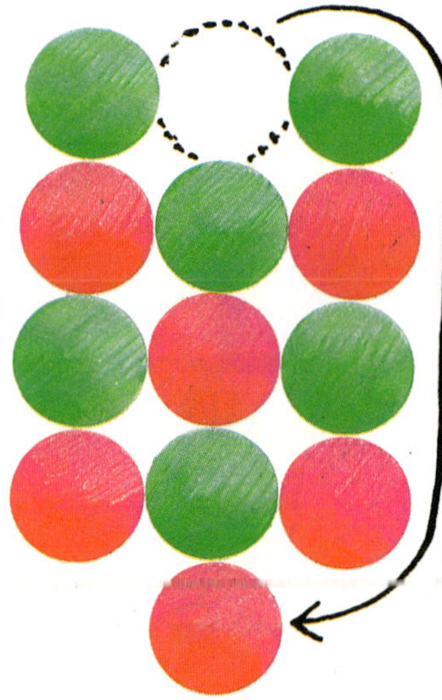

3

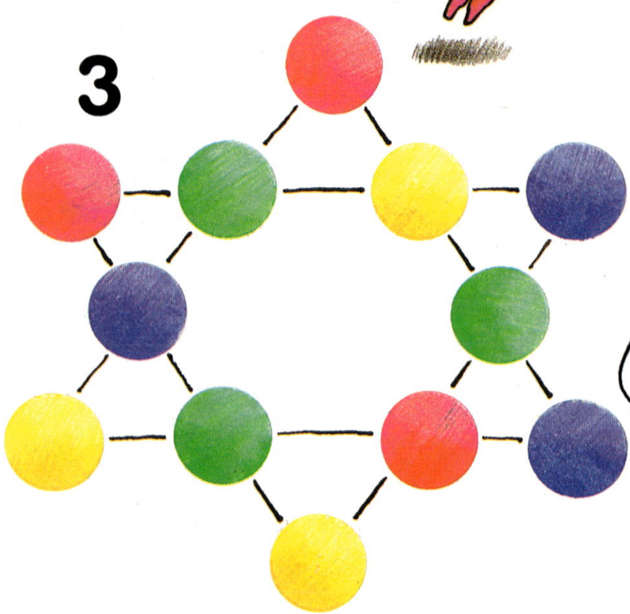

Bet this one had you fooled as well! Make a 6-pointed star like this and you will have 6 rows.

4

Fooled you?
Put the end right-hand counter on top of the yellow one like this.

5

See what I mean! Don't gnash your teeth if you couldn't do it. Try it out on a friend instead.

6

(i) Fold the paper in half.
(ii) Then open it again by pulling the ends sharply.
(iii) The paper should stand on edge and you can balance a counter in the middle.

Blockade (for two players)

The blue and red ships are enemies. Both want to stop the other from leaving port, by blocking them so they can no longer move.

How to play

- Choose to have either red or blue ships and put a counter on each of your ships to start.
- Take turns to move one counter along a line to an empty circle until one of you can no longer move

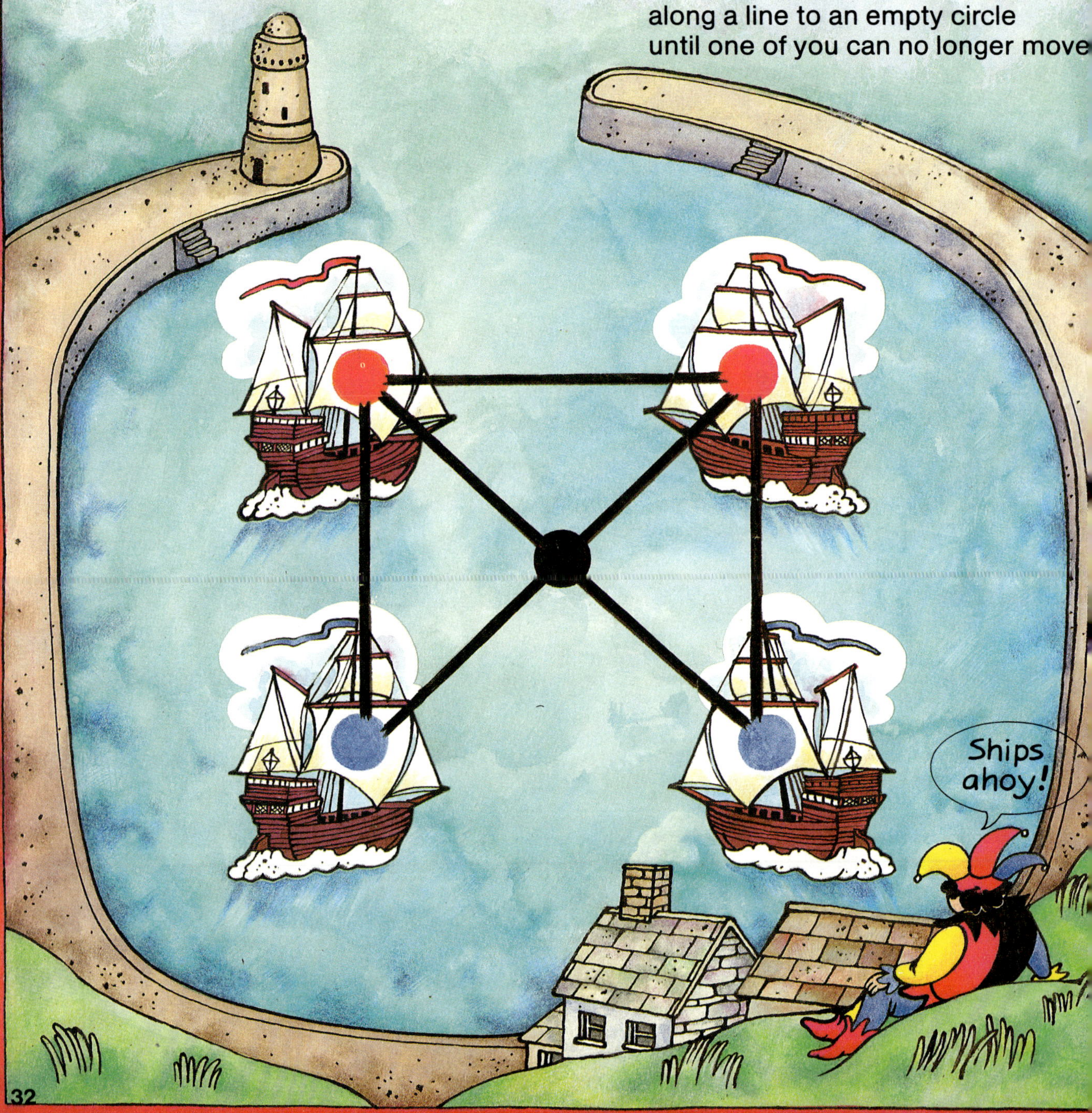